The Four Eyes...

# of Church!

The Four Eyes...

of Church!

By
Rebecca J. Fulton

**Foreword
Evangelist Rita Twiggs**

The Four Eyes of Church by Rebecca J. Fulton

ISBN: 0-9678628-0-9

CIP: 00-090894

Printed in the United States by
Morris Publishing
3212 East Highway 30
Kearney, NE 68847
1-800-650-7888

Acknowledgments

First and foremost I want to thank the Lord Jesus Christ who is the author of my destiny. It was He who allowed and permitted the individuals, the places and the events to be a part of my life.

To my husband, Donald, who has encouraged me to write this book -- and for being kind enough to let me be honest about our lives.

To my children Jeremy, his lovely wife Anne Marie and our sweet new grandbaby Tristin Tyler; to Joshua and his brand new wife Kelly; and to my baby girl Miranda, who has been very patient with me through all this writing.

To my parents Floyd & Irene who have been examples of how to live Godly lives. And to my brothers and my sister who have allowed me to use some of their lives in this book to tell my story. Also, to my husbands parents. Thank you for producing such a mighty man of God, and being great examples of how we can truly make it through the rough times.

To my church families around the world who have allowed us to be a part of their lives.

Thank You!

A special thank you to Dr. Peggy Scarborough who has been an encouragement to me and who gave me a great big push to get me motivated to write this book. Also, she so graciously edited it for me.

Also thank you to Dr. Bill Sheeks and Vicki Yohe' for endorsing my work. And a special thank you to Rita Twiggs for not only endorsing but also writing the foreword.

Thank you to Betty Boggs, Diane Herndon and Cindy Knipp for the final proofing of the book.

Thank you to Antonio Palmer for helping with the book cover.

Two final thank you's. One to JoAnn Gleason for her selfless generosity in purchasing the program needed for writing the book on for publishing.

And to Bill & Jean Wilson of World Class Cities for furnishing the funds to get the book published.

Without all these individuals, this project would not have been possible.

Thank You!

CONTENTS

Foreword
by
Evangelist Rita Twiggs

Beloved, what you are holding in your hand is not just a book, but a life. A life dedicated in service to our King. Its pages contain priceless gems of wisdom; born out of many battles fought and victories won, in areas that have heretofore been considered taboo to discuss.

Well, at long last, this sensitive but mighty

woman of God has broken the silence regarding real life in the ministry, and I am certain that her story will bring life, light, and liberty to all who take the journey with her.

Brothers and Sisters, I introduce you to the life and ministry of First Lady Rebecca Fulton. Be blessed in your reading!

Evangelist Rita Twiggs
Potter's House
Dallas, Texas
CEO - Rita Twiggs Ministries Inc.

INTRODUCTION

*W*hat qualifies me to write a book on the ministry and true life behind parsonage doors? When it comes to writing a book, please, let me use you as my guinea pigs. As for the ministry and true life accounts about what really goes on behind closed doors, I do have a few years of experience in these areas, forty-plus years to be exact.

I have struggled with writing this for some time, yet the Words from the Lord continue to pound in my soul and spirit, "Share what I've done for you and what I've brought you through, as a testimony to help others in the ministry. Let them know that they are not alone. Let them know that the feelings they are experiencing are normal, and there is light at the end of the tunnel."

Over the past twenty years I have talked with men and women in the ministry who feel they are all alone. They feel no one understands what they are going through, or no one would believe the events that are taking place in their lives. Or this, the big lie of the devil, that there is no one out there they can trust or talk to. Being in the ministry, yet rewarding as it can be, is a very lonely place. Only others in the ministry would truly understand this.

The reason I am even attempting to write this is twofold: One, as a testimony of what God has done for me and my family. All the good, bad, crazy and just unbelievable things that go on in the ministry and in the parsonage, and how we have survived and are still going strong for the Lord. And two, to let you know, you are not alone. Good things do happen, and God blesses. Yet, bad things also happen. In fact, terrible things happen to you, your family members and your churches. Yet God will use those things, good or bad, to make you the vessel only He can use. Is it an easy trip? NO! But it is a journey thousands of us have taken and are still taking. The faces and names are different, the locations cross the globe, the shapes and sizes of the homes pastors and their families live in are all different, yet very much alike. But there is one thing that you can always count on. There will always be well-meaning individuals who will let you know how to run the church, how to raise your kids, how to live a life of holiness, what to wear and what not to wear. Then, my all time favorite is when they give you money to bless you, then tell you how to spend that money.

Years ago when I was in Bible College, I used to listen to people who knew nothing about the ministry talk about how glamorous and exciting it would be to be in a full time ministry, whether it is pastoring, evangelizing, being used in the prophetic, music ministry, etc. At the time I remember thinking, especially after being raised in a pastor's home, "These people have no idea what they are talking about. As far as I knew, there was nothing glamorous or exciting about being in the ministry. There certainly wasn't anything glamorous or exciting about being a preacher's kid."

I guess this is where my journey begins.

Introduction

Going from a preacher's kid to a pastor's wife, my journey has taken me to an abundance of places, and my journey is not yet complete. But none of you need to worry, all the names have been changed to protect all pastors and their families, church members and well-meaning Christians.

So are you ready for the trip of your life? Let's go!

*****

"Train a child in the way
he [should] go:
and,
Even when old, he will not
swerve from it."
Proverbs 22:6
(CJB)

ONE

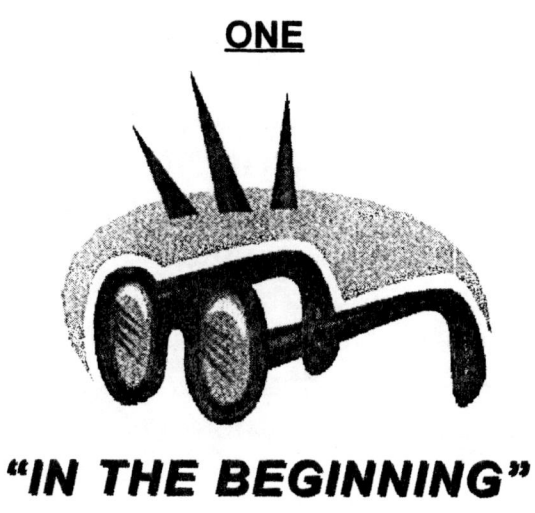

"IN THE BEGINNING"

I was born on a Sunday morning, during Sunday School, while my father was in church teaching. It seems that my destiny in life was going to be a church-related one. All I've ever known is church. In fact, when my father announced from the pulpit that I had arrived, a little girl in the church told my brother, "She's the church's baby." Talk about a prophetic word. This has been my lot in life up till now! All I know is, that it is time for this "church baby" to grow up.

Much of my childhood is blurred. I'm not for sure why that is. The only thing I can think of is that we moved around so much that I was unable to develop lasting relationships, which cause good and healthy memories. Living in two countries, seven states, ten cities and attending nineteen schools before graduating from high school doesn't help in developing lasting friendships or memories. I realize now, that this is a lifestyle that preacher's kids have no control over. Yet it is this lifestyle that we (PK's) let define our reasoning after becoming adults for why we go to church or why we stay out of church.

My family is not any different from yours. We didn't have a lot of money, although we always had enough. We always had food on the table, clothes on our backs, and a roof over our heads. I can't remember any of us ever being really sick, other than the normal childhood diseases. And as far as I could tell, each of us kids were treated the same, fairly and with love and respect.

Having three older brothers and a younger sister, I felt safe in the confines of my sibling order. My two oldest brothers were so much older than I that they had already served their time in the military, gotten married and had kids before I had reached the seventh grade. Even though my early memories of them are vague, somewhere in my spirit, those two boys could do no wrong. They were my knights in shining armor. They both had personalities that wouldn't quit, well liked by everyone, captain of just about everything in high school, from the debate team to the wrestling and football teams. And girls, they flocked to them like they were dipped in chocolate. I made a bundle of money from my brothers, (it seemed like a bundle to a six and seven-year-old), because each time they would invite a girl over, when our parents weren't home of course, they'd pay me fifty cents to keep quiet. Until now, no one ever knew that. Sorry, boys!

Then there is my brother, just older than I. He was dealt a deck of cards he was not prepared for. While my two older brothers were gone, serving their military duties, and my father was gone holding revival meetings for weeks at a time, and my mother worked the grave yard shift at the local paper mill, my brother's assignment was to baby-sit me and my little sister. He started baby-sitting at the ripe old age of nine. Here's the picture, a nine-year-old watching a five and a two-year-old from 5:00 p.m. to 2:00 a.m. every day. Then during the summer when school was out, there were times when dad was gone preaching and mom was sleeping during the day (from working all night), so he watched us all day long. What an awesome responsibility for a nine-year-old! And this went on for about four years. In today's society, Family Services probably would have stepped in and done something. But back then, especially in the ministry, you did what you had to do. It really wasn't anyone's fault. It's just the way it was.

As for my little sister, that's just what she was. She was the baby of the family, and I really didn't get to know her as a person until after I left home. Up until that time, we were two girls warring for the attention of our brothers and parents, and waiting to see who would get the best stuff or the most attention. Normal, childish behavior.

We were five kids from the same parents, yet so totally different. Sounds like a family you might know? We were all raised the same, but had different wants and needs, different goals in life, and totally different opinions on just about everything. The one thing we did have in common to my knowledge, was that none of us wanted to be in a full time ministry, the reasons being as different as each of us. I can't speak for them, but I had told myself that I would never marry a preacher and pastor a church. The older I became, the more I realized that life in a full time ministry was not the kind of life I wanted to raise my children in. I wanted to marry a good Christian man whose goal in life was to be in church every Sunday, maybe teach

"In The Beginning"

Sunday School, help out in Children's Church every other month. But pastor or evangelize, you've got to be joking! Anyone who would subject their wife and children to that kind of lifestyle had to be seriously brain dead.

I realize now that the calling of Pastor or Evangelist are two of the highest calling God can give. But I'm not talking about what I realize now, I'm talking about how I felt then, which is how a lot of preacher's kids feel.

My reasons for not wanting to be in full time ministry are too many to number, but I feel compelled to mention a few. Some of you may relate to these; some may not; but I'm going to take a chance most of you will.

The major reason I didn't want to be in the ministry was the 'moving factor'. All I can remember is moving here, moving there. I was always the new girl in school, always having to make new friends (which was difficult for me). I never could understand why we had to move so often. In most churches it's common knowledge that pastors only stay on the average of eighteen months at a church (at least that's how it was in our church). But in our case, it was a little different. My father was not just a pastor, but he was also a carpenter. This meant that while he pastored, he also built the church building. As soon as he had fully completed a church structure, we would move to the next place that needed a church built. By the time I was a teenager, I could use a hammer as well as the best carpenter around. I could pour concrete, nail the floor in place, help put the walls up, raise a truss, tar a roof, then lay the shingles. Not bad for a girl under the age of thirteen! But then the church would be built, and we would move on, leaving what few friends we had made in those few short months. On to a new school, new friends, a new church, always a new adventure!

But new adventures get old after awhile; yet life goes on!

"In The Beginning"

*****

"But He said, Leave the Children alone! Allow the little ones to come to Me, and do not forbid or restrain or hinder them for of such [as these] is the kingdom of heaven composed."
Matthew 19:14
(TAB)

TWO

"CAREFUL HOW YOU TREAT THE BABIES"

*U*nless you were raised in the home of a minister/pastor, you may not understand fully the feelings that children have concerning their parents, other ministers and people who attend church. Hopefully, the next few chapters will enlighten you and help you understand preachers' kids just a little better.

I realize that children who are raised in church may grow up and become ministers, others may not. I also realize that some children grow up who know nothing about church, surrender their lives totally to God and then enter the ministry when they become adults. Unfortunately, the ones who would best understand their children's response to events that take place in the ministry are the ones who have lived those events themselves.

For example: My husband was raised in a home that visited many churches (Seventh Day Adventist, Mormons, Jehovah's Witnesses). Yet his most vivid memories of church are when he and his family used to sit outside his grandparents home, in a little country town, and watch the people in a little Pentecostal church. Windows were open, the doors open, and people inside had hands raised and were singing the praises of the Lord. All of a sudden, someone inside the church would get excited and run out the front door and around the church. He will tell you that this was their Sunday night entertainment! Did they attend church regularly? No! Was God a vital factor in their life? No! Yet this young boy grew into a young man seeking answers. At the age of seventeen, he gave his life to the Lord, for the Lord to do whatever He chose to do with him.

Now his philosophy on how our children should act is totally different than mine. Especially when our children were younger, his guidelines and rules consisted of: "No, you can't wear shorts to church!" "No, you can't be in sports, because all the practices and games are on church nights!" "No, you can't do the things the other kids do. You've got to be the example!" (That was always my personal favorite when I was a kid.) "No, no, no, no!" On the other hand, my philosophy when the kids were little was very simple, "Let the kids be kids as long as they need to be kids." So you can imagine, our two philosophies collided on a regular basis.

I knew that I needed to raise my children to be respectful to adults and to have a respect for the House of God. My goal was always to instill in them Biblical principles so they would accept Christ as their personal Savior at a young age, then grow into responsible adults. But I never expected them to look like little adults and I never expected them to be little adults. They were children! They had two parents and two parents was all they needed!

Now this is a hard lesson for some people in the church to grasp! As in all churches, there are those people who feel their calling in life is to make sure the pastor (and everyone else in the church), knew every move that the preacher's kids make. And God forbid they see little Johnny or Susie taking something from their child or pushing their child. I had one individual lecture me for an hour, telling me the same thing over and over, "How could you do something like that? Don't you realize you're the Pastor's child? You're supposed to set the example for the rest of the children!"

There was one instance while we were pastoring in upstate New York when my youngest son was about seven years old. Church was over, and I was looking for him. It was unusual that he wasn't out front by the car waiting to go home. I had hunted for about thirty minutes when I located him in the boy's bathroom. He was crying uncontrollably and was soaking wet with perspiration. He was shaking as if he were freezing. I had never seen him like this before and I had no idea what had happened to him. For the first few minutes I just picked him up and hugged him and tried to calm him down, then my probing started. "What happened? Did someone hurt you? Are you hurting anywhere? Have you been sick? What on earth happened to cause you to be so upset?" While I was asking my son all these questions, a little boy came up and was standing behind me. Just waiting, saying nothing. I turned to him and asked, "Do you know what happened here?" All the boy said was, "I'm waiting for him to apologize." Now I was totally stumped. "Apologize for what?"

"He took my ball from me, and I told my dad. My dad is waiting in the car for me, but he told me he had just had a long talk with him, and he was ready to apologize."

Finally my son, barely being able to speak more than two words at a time, told me the boys were playing football. He tackled the boy and ran with the ball. This story was confirmed by nearly thirty other children and adults. Yet when the story got back to the other boy's father, it had changed somewhat. So taking it upon himself, this caring individual proceeded to tell my seven-year-old the following, "You are going to grow up and become a thief. God will never forgive you. You need to fall on your knees right now and ask God to forgive you. People will never trust you, and your word will mean nothing. If you do not say you're sorry, you're going to grow up and carry this guilt around your whole life."

You might as well have taken a gun and shot the kid! Can you imagine telling a child, "God will never forgive you!" And "You're going to carry this guilt around your whole life." It's hard enough to live in a glass house, and it's the pits having every-thing you do put under a microscope, but give me a break! If you have a problem with my children bring them to me and let me deal with them, I am the parent, not you! And secondly, never drop such heavy condemnation on a child!

Needless to say, by this time I was fuming! Of course, I made my son apologize to the boy. But before I let the young man leave, I asked him, "Wouldn't you like to apologize also?" Now, can you guess what his answer was?" You're right! "NO!"

I sent my son to the car and walked the other boy to his car, where his parents waited. I told them what had just happened. Also, I explained to them the correct account of what had transpired between the two boys. Then I proceeded to tell them, with all the love I could muster, never to verbally attack my son or any other child again. I also told the father I expected him to apologize to my son for his actions. (When I was a child that never happened, because adults were never wrong.) You know something Christians, it's O.K. to admit you're wrong and you've made a mistake to a child. Do you know what it does to a child when he feels he is always wrong and always has to take the blame for everything that happens? Think about it! How would it make you feel?

Over the past twenty years of ministry, I've only had three incidents where I've felt the "She-Bear" come out of me to protect my young! This event was one of them.

Usually my husband handled every other

incident in a more professional manner! If we did-n't feel our children were facing life-threatening, life-altering events, we let them handle most of their own fights. Getting along, solving problems or fighting, kids do it all the time, and an hour later they're best friends again. Usually we never got involved in that sort of kid stuff.

Just remember, the pastor's children have parents. Respect them as parents, just as you would want others to respect you as your children's parents. Do you know how confusing it is for one child to have two-hundred parents? Everyone telling them a different way to do the same thing! When I let myself think about it, I'm surprised to see how many preachers' kids become functional adults! Above all, don't take your frustrations toward the pastor out on his children. If you have a problem with the pastor, take it up with him. Leave the children out of it. I don't know how many times I was invited over to someone's house to play with their children only to be drilled about why my father did this, or why he did that! "I don't know, ask him!"

A word of warning! Be careful how you treat children whose parents are in ministry. You don't know what they've been through. You don't know if they fully understand the pressure they are under. You don't know what's going on behind the closed doors of the church parsonage. A kind word and a smile can go a long way.

Yes, I know some preachers' kids can be devils: but hey, some of you have a few devils of your own running around the church. Remember, what goes around comes around. You may find you need someone to say a kind word to one of yours one day!

"Careful How You Treat The Babies"

*****

"No disaster will happen to you, no calamity will come near your tent; for He will order His angels to care for you and guard you wherever you go."
Psalms 91:10 & 11
(CJB)

THREE

"PARSONAGES FROM THE DARK SIDE"

Many of the homes we lived in when I was a child were unbelievable. I remember wondering if everyone lived in that kind of house? It didn't take me long to figure out that the answer to that question was **NO!**

Everyone was not as blessed as we were to live in a house with holes in the walls, that is if we had walls. Nearly every house we lived in was not quite finished. You know, it needed a little fixing up!

Maybe a new window put in, or a little wall put up or a door hung, and it could always use a fresh coat of paint. But the thing I enjoyed the most were the carpets (when we had them). I remember brown and orange carpets, brown and tan carpets, brown and darker brown carpet, but my favorite was a carpet in the parsonage we lived in in New Mexico. The color of this carpet was that lovely color of men's long-underwear. You know what I'm referring too, that not quite white, and not quite gray, and not quite yellow, just that not-quite-color! Yet it wasn't so much the color that stands out in my mind. It was the big burn holes. There were about three of them, two feet by three feet. How they got there, I never found out. All I knew was that it was ugly.

My mother decided to cover them with throw rugs. So with her own money, she purchased three nice little throw rugs to cover the holes. When the ladies' ministry found out, they threw a fit. Now you must remember, at that time, the "Ladies' Auxiliary" furnished the parsonages, and in some areas still do.

This group of ladies, marched into the house and removed the throw rugs and boldly stated that, "Those in the ministry should live a humble existence." Excuse me, I can be very humble, thank you! With the throw rugs on the floor! If you want me to be humble, you set the example! Let me burn some holes in your carpet and see how humble you are.

It was these same women who brought us a pounding (food to make sure we didn't starve to death in the parsonage with the burn holes in the carpet), consisting of a hundred-pound sack of potatoes. We had mashed potatoes, fried potatoes, boiled potatoes, baked potatoes, potato soup, potato pancakes, french-fried potatoes and potato patties. Never once did they bring flour, salt, pepper, oil or milk to make gravy. Never once did they bring meat to go with the potatoes. Were we grateful for the potatoes? You bet, but in the mind of a child, it sure would have been nice to experience the enjoyment of a full three-course meal, and maybe one meal when the pounding arrived could have included a dessert. By the way, if anyone is wanting to send me one, for all those I missed as a child, I love pecan pies and double chocolate cake. That's just in case inquiring minds are wanting to know.

Twice in my childhood I recall not having even potatoes. As a family, we knelt down at the dinner table, fully set with dishes, and prayed that the Lord would provide supper for that evening. Both times, someone came to the door with fully prepared meals from salad to main course and even dessert. Not once in my life did I ever go hungry. God was faithful to provide every meal.

Now about the fixer-uppers. There are two that come to mind, one in Alaska and the other in Washington state. At both of these parsonages, which by the way were unfinished, my sister and I slept in the basement. In the parsonage in Washington, I at first slept in the living room, but that didn't last long because we had to use it for a Sunday School room. Then I moved to the attic, but that didn't work either. So the basement became the bedroom for my sister and me. Well, at least one room in the basement. Our room had one door. Outside that door was the basement from **HELL!** Hollywood could have come and filmed all their horror flicks there. You know those movies when they open the dreaded basement door and look down in the darkness, and you're sitting in your living room or in the movie theater screaming, "Don't go down there. He's down there. The monster is going to get you!" That was this basement. It had one single light bulb hanging from an extension cord in the middle of the room about two-thirds down the stairs, which loomed in the middle of the room. To turn the light on or off, you had to flick the switch on the light bulb socket itself, and run to the room, praying you didn't get caught by whatever lurked in the darkness.

Once while lying on the bed and looking at the bare cement floor, I saw a strange insect crawling across the floor. It was about an inch long, white in color and puffed up like a small balloon. I had no idea what it was, so I took a glass and captured it so I could show someone the next day. "Where did this creature come from?" "From under my bed!" What was this puffed up insect? That was my first encounter with a queen termite. That was one house I was thankful to move from.

The other parsonage to remember was in Alaska. It was very similar to the basement from hell house, except this basement, unlike the other, had little windows at the top of the basement, just above the ground. These windows were not in very solid. When the wind would blow, it would whistle through them. On those long winter nights in Alaska, those sounds in that dark cold basement would keep my sister and me under the covers until someone would come down and rescue us so we could get ready for school the next morning.

One night around 2 a.m. the wind was blowing like never before. The whistling started in a low, evil moaning whistle, the kind that makes the hair on the back of your neck stand on ends. After about five minutes of this eerie wailing, the wind picked up a piece of wood and flung it through our bedroom window, then sucked it back out the window. Our bed was covered with glass. Now instead of the wind wailing through the window, it was my sister and me who were doing the wailing.

You may not have experienced the basement from **HELL** or had only potatoes for nourishment, yet if you were raised in the ministry, I'm sure you have a horror story or two of your own to tell. If you're new to the ministry, just hang on, you'll get a few stories under your belt soon enough.

Yet through it all, our family was together and now I can look back and can appreciate what the Lord has done for me. We've all come a long way, and it's only by the grace and mercy of the Lord we've survived. **BUT WE HAVE SURVIVED!** Thank God the parsonages we live in now are not the homes no one else wants to live in and they are not fixer-uppers. If they were, we'd be hiring a carpenter, because my husband does not know how to swing a hammer.

If you are living in your basement from **HELL** now and your diet consists of potatoes alone, God is about to take you from the basement to the penthouse and set a banquet of the finest foods before you. Just be faithful where you are. It will only last for a season.

"Parsonages From The Dark Side"

*****

"So she left the place where she was...for where you go I will go, and where you lodge I will lodge..."
Ruth 1:7a & 16B
(TAB)

FOUR

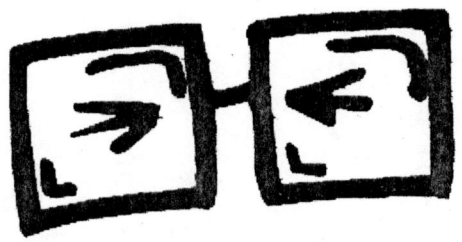

"WE'RE MOVING AGAIN?"

*M*oving can be a very stress-ful time for a child. It was probably the most stress-ful time that I can recall in my childhood. It would begin when it was announced from the pulpit that my father would be resigning the church and we would be moving on. Several times I didn't know we would be moving until it was announced from the pulpit. SURPRISE! SURPRISE!

In an earlier chapter I told how my father was not only a pastor, but also a carpenter. This was a gift and talent that the church used to their fullest advantage. While my father would pastor a church, he would also build the church building. Beautiful churches, complete with sanctuary, Sunday School rooms, fellowship hall, landscaping and parking lots.

Pastoring a church is stressful enough for pastors and their families, but when you throw a building program in it, life becomes almost unbearable.

Needless to say, after each building was finished, and I would think we would be able to enjoy the new facilities, it would be time to move on. I went to nineteen schools before I graduated from high school, sometimes going to two and three schools a year. I used to wonder what it would be like to stay in the same city and go to the same school and grow up with the same kids from grade school through high school, until I met a girl who had lived in the same house since she had been born, knew the same kids forever and all she wanted was to travel and see the world. It was then I decided, that you have to make the best of whatever is dealt you in life. Don't complain about what you don't have, but instead thank God for what you've got.

I think the hardest move for me as a child was when we moved from Washington State to

New Mexico State. I was in the eleventh grade, with seven weeks to go before the school year was out for the summer. That was the longest I had been in one school, and I really liked it there. But my father took a church in Roswell, New Mexico, and we had to go. Something inside of me seemed to die. I didn't want to go! I shouldn't have to go! It wasn't fair! Why couldn't someone make this madness stop? I silently cried all the way to New Mexico. If it hadn't been for my oldest brother, driving this huge white truck (lovingly called the "white elephant") with all our belongings in it, I don't believe I could have survived. Because he used every means possible he could think of to keep my sister and I laughing. That was the only good memory I had of that move.

When we got to our new home, I entered a new school. I was overweight and dressed differently than everyone else in the school. It was the first school I had attended in which each nationalities stayed completely to themselves. The whites didn't mix with the blacks; the blacks didn't mix with the Spanish; the Spanish didn't mix with the Indians. The only time they agreed on anything was just before we had arrived. They had all gotten together and tried to burn the school down during a teachers work day, with all the teachers inside! I knew I was totally out of my element.

Several of the classes that I was taking in Washington State were not even offered in this new school. So I had to make up full semesters of two classes in only seven weeks. One class I had to do a full term paper, which the class had been working on the whole semester, and all I was given was a topic. Thank God for my mother! While I was in school, she would go to the library and check out the books I would need for the report. After school, I would write the paper, then while I was in school, she would proofread it. I would come home and redo what needed to be done. While I was in school, she would type it. If it hadn't been for her, I would not have passed that class. Just in case you're interested, I got the highest grade in the class. Even I was shocked! In the two classes I had to make up, I got B's. But it was then I decided, I wasn't going to move any more. I wasn't sure how I was going to accomplish it, but I wasn't moving again!

That summer, I did every odd job I could find, from baby-sitting to car washes. I filled out an application to go to Bible college, where they had a High School and College combined. I was accepted! I got my driver's license at the age of 15 and left home at 16 and went to Bible College in Fresno, California. I completed my senior year and graduated there, I also completed my college there. Since the age of 16, I've not lived at home. Do I recommend that for everyone? Absolutely, NOT! But for me, at that time, it was something I had to do. I'm sure that if my parents had felt that I wasn't ready for it, they would have fought harder to make me stay, or they would have just put their foot down and just said "no." But with their parental and Godly wisdom, they allowed me to go.

Even though I can't look back and remember any friends from my childhood, and some places fade from memory, that's O.K., because I wouldn't trade my life or family for anything. I needed certain events to happen in my life to prepare me for what the Lord had for me to do as an adult.

If your children are having a hard time with the moves you've decided to make, don't be so hard on them. They're dealing with their own sense of loss. Their sense of adventure may not be the same as yours. Moving sometimes can be fun; but after a while, it grows old. Friends and memories are important, as you will find it will also be important to you when you find yourself growing old, with no one you can truly call your friend.

For those of you who are in a move right now, here's a word of advice that my mother gave me when we first started out in the ministry. "Make your house a home as quickly as you can for your children's sake. Get their room set up, the pictures on the walls, and the house in order so their lifestyle and schedules won't be messed up for too long." It's something I've done for more than twenty years. Within three days of any move we've made, you can come into my house and it will look like we've lived there for years. Why? Because my kids are important to me, and so should yours be to you.

You may want to move, pastor, but remember, you're not just moving to another city and another house. You're moving a family and a home! And to women and children, that is a big deal.

"We're Moving Again?"

*****

"These six things the Lord hates...A heart that manufactures wicked thoughts and plans...a false witness who breathes out lies (even under oath}, and who sows discord among his brethren."
Proverbs 6:16a, 18a & 19
(TAB)

FIVE

"THE ART OF MANIPULATION"

*T*he things you learn as a child and the experiences that teach you about life are invaluable to you when you become a teenager. Preachers' kids are a unique breed. We learn things at a young age that can sometimes help us in life, yet also be hazardous to us. There are characteristics that are common to kids in the ministry. We learn them when we are young, and use them when we become teens. Hopefully we outgrow the unhealthy ones when we become adults, keeping and using only those that will benefit the Kingdom of God.

What characteristics am I talking about? Let's see, where should I begin? These characteristics we didn't just learn from our parents. Let's give them a break here. We learned a great deal from guest ministers, but mostly we learned them from watching the people who sat on the pews. That's right, we learned a great deal from you, and you were good teachers.

One time I watched a family from a church several hundred miles away from where we lived approach my father to come pastor their church. My father said, "No," yet they continued to work on him. They offered this, then they offered that. They pleaded and begged. Little by little, they wore him down until he agreed to go. And of course, they needed a new church building. I realize now that what they did was manipulate my father by their offers to settle for something he may not have really wanted.

So I thought that if they could little by little get him to do somethings he really didn't want to do, maybe I could too. So the big day came for us to meet the church for the first time as a family. They had planned a big potluck dinner and the church was excited about our coming. We dressed in our best Sunday clothes and drove the two-hour drive through the mountains to church. My plan was that I was not going to eat at that potluck, I was going to eat blueberry pancakes. So I started on my dad as soon as we got in the car. By the time we got to our destination, he had agreed to get me blueberry pancakes. Whether it was to shut me up or whether I had made him feel bad for moving us again, I'm not quite for sure. All I knew is that I had succeeded in getting him to agree to blueberry pancakes.

He preached that morning and it was finally time for the potluck. Yet in my mind it was time for pancakes. Everyone tried to get me to eat. I refused. Now I was very polite about it by saying, "No thank you. My dad is going to get me pancakes." My mother tried to get me to eat. I refused. My dad tried to get me to eat. I refused. I told everyone, "No thank you. I'm going to eat blueberry pancakes!" I kept on until we finally left the potluck and went to a pancake house for blueberry pancakes. Inside of me I knew I had just gotten my way by manipulating the situation and people. A part of me felt like I had just conquered the world. Yet a part of me felt very bad while I was eating those pancakes. I remember the look on my father's face -- a mixture of anger, hurt and frustration. I did not understand what my father was going through that day. All I knew is that I wanted pancakes, and I got them. (Just like the people at this church got, in getting my father to agree to come to their church.) I was in the ninth grade at that time, old enough to know better, but just old enough to know when to start using that little tactic called manipulation.

I see children use it all the time. The scary thing is that they are getting younger and younger and are using it more wisely than ever before. I see children four, five, and six years of age who are masters of manipulation. Most people don't put up with a child screaming, yelling, and throwing a tantrum because they recognize right away that he is trying to get his own way.

For instance, there was this one four-year-old boy in a church my husband and I were pastoring in California. He refused to go to Sunday School or Children's Church. At that time I just happened to be his Sunday School teacher and also the Children's Church teacher. His mother would bring him sobbing softly (playing on his mothers sympathy). As soon as she would begin to leave, he would start screaming and kicking and throwing one of the best fits I've ever seen. But that wasn't the best part. He would stick his fingers down his throat and make himself throw-up. I had seen him do it several times before, but was not in the position to do anything about it. This time though, he was being left in my care. I told this totally frustrated mother just to leave him. I said, "He will be O.K. and so will you."

I told her that his crying wouldn't interrupt my class at all. She left, very hesitantly, but relieved that someone else was going to deal with him. He screamed for about two minutes then it was time for the fingers down the throat trick. Immediately I picked him up and announced to him, "You throw-up, and I will spoon feed it back into you." He looked at me to see if I was serious, and immediately his attitude changed. He knew he had met his match. He never once threw a fit again in class. Now he tried it with his mother a few times. Then she asked me what I had done. After about three weeks of helping the child see the error of his ways, that was the sweetest little four-year-old around.

So you see, it's easier to deal with the loud, obnoxious ones. It's the quiet and polite ones, like me, who become dangerous when they become adults if their problems are not dealt with early.

Thank God my manipulative spirit was turned around to inspire people to come to the Lord and to encourage them to live Godly lives, instead of using it solely for my own benefit. I can't imagine living a life just for me, me, me. God is nowhere within a hundred miles of that kind of attitude.

If you see your child, or your teenager manipulating or being a con-artist (which is another common characteristic among church people), find out where this spirit is coming from. Are they following someone else's footsteps or are they following in your footsteps? Whichever the case may be, ask God to help you change the situation so that your children can have Godly examples to follow. Remember, children learn from examples, whether it is yours or a church member.

The saying, "The youth of today are the church of tomorrow," is very true. But also is the saying, "The nut doesn't fall far from the tree." What type of church are we setting into motion now? Your child may someday be someone's Pastor. Are they going to be in the ministry for what they can get, or what they can give?

"The Art Of Manipulation"

*****

"...Work out your own sal-
vation with fear
and trembling..."
Philippians 2:12b
(KJ)

SIX

"YES, I HAVE CONVICTIONS!
I THINK?"

*N*ow you may say, "I don't have small children. All of mine are in college or out of the house." Well then, all your worries are over. Aren't they? Guess again! Thank God for all those who develop a true relationship with the Lord while they are young and carry it into their adult years. The problem with preachers' kids are that, while growing up, they live under mama and daddy's convictions and rules. This is not bad, but few are given the opportunity to develop their own convictions. So when they leave the house and are out from under their parents constant care and eye sight, they are not for sure what they believe or how they feel about certain issues. Now I could tell you how my parents felt about certain issues. I knew my dad's opinion on church, money and sex. Yet were my parents' convictions my convictions? Sadly to say, I was married and had children of my own and was in full-time ministry with my husband before I finally developed certain convictions of my own.

For instance, I was not allowed to wear makeup or jewelry or go to movies. I could not attend high school ball games, yet the boys were captain of all the ball teams. I often wondered if there were a different set of standards for my sister and me than there were for the boys. I was not allowed to attend any prom or dances. I only dated when there was a group of kids going, usually eight to twelve kids and Lord have mercy, it wasn't called a date. The boys were called friends, but not boy friends!

Needless to say, when I left home, I had to learn what was right for me, without compromising my Christian principles. That process took me several years. I know my parents spent many sleepless nights praying for me, as I had heard them do for my brothers when they left home. Thank God for praying parents.

Many preachers' kids that I have known, left home and totally went away from the teachings of the church and their parents. They got caught up in things that led them completely away from God. This happens more than we'd really like to admit. After seeing the things their parents go through, after having their childhood robbed from them, after seeing the hypocrisy in the church, some come to the realization that if being poor and living in shacks, and living out of care packages was the life of a Christian, that it was no life for them. Anyway, think about it, most teenagers live in the NOW and can't comprehend what good could possibly come from this type of lifestyle. So they abort the calling on their lives just before they receive what God has for them.

I have a brother whom I've heard say more than once, "Most Christians look like they've lost their best friend and a few of them could use a little makeup." Out of five children, this brother turned away from the church instead of toward it, because of the lifestyle of certain so-called Christians. Tragic as it is, many Christians will give an account of their actions and attitudes done toward preachers and their families in the name of Christianity.

I remember the first movie I went to. I sat in the auditorium and prayed the rapture wouldn't happen while I was sitting there. But I was less fearful of the rapture happening than I was my father finding out. I could deal with God, but please God don't let my father find out. For my father, it was wrong to go to movies', and I respect him for his beliefs. Yet I never knew why it was wrong. I had never read a scripture in the Bible that said, "Thou shalt not go to the movies." I just knew that you were going to Hell if you did. So I thought!

Then revelation hit me between the eyes one day. My husband and I took our first church in the country of Panama. We pastored a small military church in the middle of the jungle. There were four military posts that were strategically placed in different parts of the jungle on either side of the Panama Canal. The only communication with the outside world was the telephone and one Southern Command Military TV station, which only aired the reject shows from the United States that didn't make it on the air as regular shows here in the States. And of course, it got episodes of a popular soap opera called General Hospital, the only problem was that the episodes were a year old. The TV programming began airing at 3:00 p.m. in the afternoon and went off the air at 10:00 p.m. Could you get hooked on the TV? Not hardly! The reception was so bad most of the time you couldn't see the picture anyway. So the only other means of entertainment was a three-lane bowling alley, drinking, drugging, having affairs and a family movie theater.

When you have 35,000 military personnel and three lanes of bowling, how often do you think, you get to bowl? And being the pastor of the church, drinking, drugging and having affairs were out! So I really did some soul-searching about this movie issue. This was a family theater and showed only "G" and "PG" movies. We could preach against movies and have the kids out on the streets, or we could let the kids have a place to hang out that was much safer than having them on the streets getting into trouble and becoming hooked on drugs and alcohol. Suddenly I realized that it wasn't the movies that would send me to Hell. It was my attitude and the condition of my heart. By now, I was old enough to know what I should watch and what I shouldn't. I knew that if I filled my spirit man with garbage, garbage would eventually come out.

If God has told you not to go to movies, you better obey the voice of the Lord for your life. There must be some reason He doesn't want you there. But just because He doesn't allow you to go, don't belittle someone else who does go. Their convictions may fall in an area that you don't have a problem with.

Do I go to movies? You bet! For the past twenty plus years we have lived away from our families. So on Thanksgiving Day and Christmas Day, we have a family tradition of picking a comedy movie for the family to go to and we sit and laugh for a while. Hey, a lot of you are with your families on the holidays. We have not had that luxury! We opted to laugh at a funny movie rather than sit at home and cry thousands of miles away from our families.

Be sensitive to what the Lord is saying to your heart. He will only convict you of the things that are not good for your life and your ministry. Just because you're a Levite and can't cut your hair doesn't mean that the one standing next to you can't cut theirs. My mother told me a story of when she went to Bible College back in the 1930's. She had beautiful long black hair and she liked to wear it down around her shoulders. But when she got to the college, they made her cut her hair and roll it up in a small roll that fit tightly around the back of her neck and the sides of her head. She cried for weeks because they cut her hair short and rolled it up to make it look long. One day in prayer, the Lord told her, "There are a lot of women who have long hair on their heads, but have short hair in their hearts." So make sure that what you are doing on the outward for everyone to see goes along with what is going on on the inside.

God doesn't care what's on the outside. You can wear dresses with hems down to the floor and a collar up to your ears, be as plain as can be with hair wadded up in the highest bun on the top of your head and walk straight into Hell if your heart is not right.

*****

"By this shall all {men} know that you are My disciples, if you love one another."

John 13:15

(TAB)

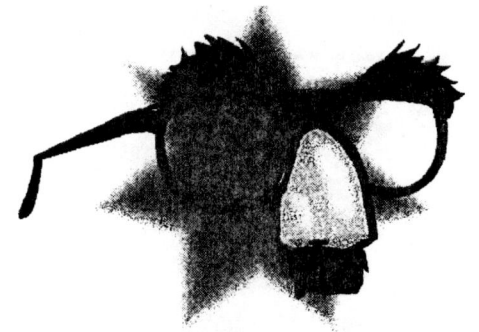

SEVEN

"THEY SAID THEY WERE CHRISTIANS!"

Being raised in the ministry should have prepared me for what was to come as my husband and I began our own ministry. But quite the contrary! What I knew of the ministry up until that time was seen and experienced through the eyes and emotions of a child. It is very different being the minister yourself. Thankfully, my parents did a fantastic job of protecting me. I often tell people that I lived a very sheltered life. I honestly believed that all Christians loved everyone and that I would grow up and live in a nice little white house with a white picket fence and have 2.3 children who would always stay clean and never give anyone any heartache. Boy, was my idea of a Christian lifestyle and the ministry shattered.

It was a shock to me to realize that all Christians didn't believe the same way that we did. And can you believe it, many of them interpreted the Bible differently than we did? Suddenly the things that seemed so simple before became quite complicated. Where were those people (my parents) who had taught me everything I knew? Mom and Dad, where were you now? I know that it may have appeared that I didn't think you knew too much when I was a teen, but now...you seem to be two of the most intelligent people I know. Many times I've called my parents and asked for advice over the years. They may not have had the answers, but at least they could pray.

It didn't take long to exhaust all my childish wisdom on the easy problems that arose in our early ministry. Now the more difficult issues started to arise. Now these were adultery, divorce, child abuse, teen pregnancy, rape, incest, bitterness, anger, hate. Then problems arose that I had never heard of before. These were multiple marriages. I'm not talking about one divorce. I'm talking about being divorced five and six times from the same partner, with a partner in between each marriage. Or how about fathers who assaulted their children with sledge hammers? Or how about fifteen and sixteen year old girls who seduced only the married men in the church? And the married men who fell for it! The list seemed to become endless.

Early in our ministry a woman came to the church one Sunday afternoon. She said she was from a church in Los Angeles and was traveling to a healing ministry in Michigan somewhere. We were pastoring in Las Vegas, approximately a four hour drive from Los Angeles. We were familiar with the church she was from, so it seemed safe to invite her into our home for the afternoon until the evening service started.

Once we were settled inside, with a cool glass of iced tea, she began to tell us why she wanted to get to this healing ministry. She had ovarian cancer and wanted the minister there to pray for her. The more she talked, the more uneasy we became. Something wasn't quite right with her. She asked if we would pray for her before she left. (We could tell she needed prayer, but is wasn't for cancer). She wanted us to lay hands on the place where the sickness was! My husband looked at me and I looked at him. "My God, what is she asking?" This was too much for my young inexperienced husband, so he excused himself to go to the office to study for the night sermon and left me alone with her and our ten-month-old baby.

Immediately after he left, she wanted to pray. She proceeded to lie down on my living room floor, lift up her dress and grab her private area and begin praying at the top of her lungs. She laid there for forty-five minutes shouting and screaming and groaning (at least that's what I called it, although she might have called it praying). When she was done, she got up, collected her belongings and left. I watched her walk down the road singing at the top of her lungs. She never attended the evening service and we never saw her again. After that experience, I realized that there were a lot of strange people who called themselves Christians. **(It would have been nice to have had some of those minor details explained to me before going into full time ministry).**

Especially when two weeks later a gentleman called at two o'clock in the morning and just had to meet with the pastor. When he got there, the dog was barking, the baby was crying, and I wasn't too happy myself. I took the dog and the baby in the bedroom and left the door cracked just enough to hear what was going on. He had just come down from Boulder Dam and had to return as soon as possible because the aliens were coming at five in the morning to take him to see Jesus. He just wanted to make sure he was baptized before they took him. You should have seen the look on my husband's face. My husband asked, "You're not serious, are you?" "Oh, yes!" The man was quite serious. Well then, the only natural question was, "Where at two in the morning could he be baptized?" That's right! The bathtub! He told my husband he didn't mind being baptized in the tub because this was an emergency. At that point my husband realized he had to get this man out of our home as soon as possible. So as not to get him too upset, he defused the situation as tactful as possible and said, "You know, you probably misunderstood what the aliens told you. I didn't hear anything about them coming to take us to see Jesus! Why don't you wait until tomorrow and come back in the day time? We'll do a baptism then because a baptism is something special and you don't want to miss that by being baptized in a bathtub!"

He seemed to be satisfied with that answer. They had a short prayer and he left. The remainder of the night both of us just stared at the ceiling, wondering what we had gotten ourselves into.

If you haven't encountered a "Strange Christian" yet in your ministry, you've probably only been in the ministry for a day or two. Trust me. They are out there. And for all the truly sincere believers, it will always be the "Strange" ones that stand out in your memory.

You may be at that stage of your ministry where you're lying in the bed wondering, "What have we gotten ourselves into? Take heart. Thousands of God's chosen have wondered those same words and God has kept all of them. And what's great about God, He always seems to shine the brightest in the strangest places.

"The Said They Were Christians!"

*****

"That He might present it to Himself a glorious church, not having spot, or wrinkle, or any such thing; but that it should be holy and without blemish."
Ephesians 5:27
(KJ)

EIGHT

"STRANGE THINGS HAPPEN IN CHURCH? NAW!"

I've read hundreds of books on how people think it should be in the ministry and how you are supposed to act in the ministry. But I've never read a book on what actually happens when you're out there on the field. In fact, when I read some of the books, I wondered if some of those people had actually been in the ministry.

The stories you will read in this book are all true. They are not made up. They are not fiction.

I couldn't even imagine these things. I used to think, "No one would ever believe me if I told them these stories. I can hardly believe them myself." But they are all true.

Part of the loneliness in the ministry is that so many unbelievable things happen and you feel no one will believe you. You struggle to find answers on your own and very seldom do. Many times I wondered, "How can I be a normal wife and mother and have some kind of normal lifestyle like other young couples? How can my children have a normal family life when everything around them seems to be so abnormal? How can I have the answers for everyone's problem when for the most part, I don't even understand what the problem is. Then when I did understand the problem, I wondered if there was even an answer for it in the Bible.

Learn a valuable lesson here and now, one that took me many years to learn. **YOU WON'T HAVE THE ANSWER TO EVERYONE'S PROBLEMS! DON'T EVEN TRY!** You will drive yourself crazy and everyone around you crazy trying. It's not your place to solve their problems. It's God's! Give them Godly counsel and advice, teach them to read the Word and find scriptures appropriate for their situation, then instruct them to pray. As long as they remain dependent upon you to solve all their problems, they will remain dysfunctional "Christians." When they remain dysfunctional, the church remains dysfunctional. Teach them the answers to all their problems lies in a personal, intimate relationship with Jesus Christ.

When the strange, bizarre times come, and they will, just turn toward Heaven and say, "This one's for you God."

One such strange and bizarre time was in a church in Las Vegas. My husband was unhappy because the church did not seem to be growing in attendance as fast as he thought it should be growing. So he went down to the rescue mission and asked if anyone would like to go to church with him on Sunday. A few said "yes,' but by the time Sunday had come, he had an entire bus full of people who came.

When he arrived at the church that Sunday morning the bus was full of men and women from the rescue mission and it was just in time for Sunday School. All the teachers were in place. Everyone was in their Sunday best's. The scent of cologne and perfume filled the air in the sanctuary.

Then without warning, through the church doors burst in twenty-three dirty, unwashed, smelly, unshaven, half-dressed men and women, carrying rolled-up knap-sacks and toten' old beat-up backpacks. Two of the women had babies, and the babies were screaming at the top of their lungs (only because they were hungry).

The majority of them sat in the back of the church all grouped together. A few decided they wanted to sit among the people; and so they did! They climbed over seats, nudged past women in their beautiful dresses and men in their nice tailored suits. (It's amazing how you can visibly watch Christians develop an attitude right before your eyes).

Finally everyone was seated, which took about ten minutes. The Sunday School teacher began. She began very slowly because one of the men from the rescue mission was sitting right in front of her and he smelled so bad that you could smell him all the way to the back of the church. So with tissue in hand, held as close to her nose as she could get and still be able to talk, she more than likely taught her most unforgettable lesson.

Why? Thanks for asking! During the lesson the two screaming babies from the mission were finally quieted by their mothers who removed one side of their clothing and revealed their...Well, the babies were hungry. What did you expect? Then came the burping, belching, scratching, and the varying volumes of other types of air being released during the quietest moments during the lesson.

By now the church members were using their bulletins as fans. Everyone was fidgeting in their seats and several were excusing themselves to use the rest room. But the best was yet to come!

Now you would have thought that the teacher, who was visibly shaken, would have deviated from her method of teaching for at least this one Sunday. But alas, she did not! So what transpired next is one for the books!

As she did every Sunday, she opened the class up for questions and answers. Guess whose hand was the first up? That's right, the man on the front row, our visitor from the rescue mission. Now he didn't realize that the questions were supposed to relate to the lesson just taught or that he was supposed to wait to be called on to speak. As his hand was going up, he was asking his question, "Would you like to hear me play my flute?" At that moment, you could have knocked the Sunday School teacher over with a feather.

Well, I can say one thing for this man, he was consistent. As he was asking his question, he was making his way to the platform. Somewhere from his seat on the front row to the platform he produced a very large wood flute, pulling it from under the oversized, cape-like coat he was wearing. Almost immediately upon arrival to the platform, he began to play "SNAKE CHARMING MUSIC!" At that moment you could have knocked the rest of us over with feathers.

My husband, who by now had been approached by every councilman, elder, teacher and member of the church, was praying frantically, asking God to help him get out of this mess. Suddenly the big announcement came. The man playing the flute announced that he was...."JESUS!"

It was the first time that this church had ever had Jesus show up in one of their services. With that announcement, my husband ran to the platform, motioned for the piano player to begin playing There is Power in the Blood. He told the congregation to begin praying while he began to plead the Blood of Jesus Christ over that service. About the second verse of the song, the man with the flute cursed and ran out the front door of the church, followed by eleven of his buddies. The other eleven ran to the altar and gave their hearts to the Lord.

Strange and bizarre? You bet! But the Lord saw the innocence of my husband's heart and turned what could have been a complete disaster into eleven souls being snatched from the pit of hell.

Remember, God shines the brightest in those strange and bizarre events of your life.

"Strange Things Happen In Church? Naw!"

＊＊＊＊＊

"The Lord is nigh unto them that are of a broken heart; and saveth such as be of a contrite spirit. Many are the afflictions of the righteous: but the Lord delivereth him out of them all."

Psalms 34:18 & 19

(KJ)

NINE

"THE DEVIL TRIED BUT FAILED"

$\mathcal{T}$ hroughout the years the Lord has taken care of us. No matter what the situation has been, no matter how crazy it seems to have gotten, we have never gone without. Not without a roof over our heads, not without food on our table or clothes on our backs. He has never let us down, even when it seemed like He had.

Maybe you've never been there, and I can hear you saying, "Hopefully I won't." But if you manage to escape this growing period of your life, you will have missed one of the most valuable and intimate times with Christ that you will have ever known.

How much does Christ love you? He loves you enough to take you through the valley of the shadow of death. He loves you enough to be there when your world is falling apart. He loves you enough to pick up the pieces of your shattered lives. He loves you enough to answer your questions when you ask, "Why?"

Now have you been there? I thought so. It's a hard place to be, isn't it? You're probably recalling that event, that fight, that accident, that abuse, that sickness, etc., right now. You may be going through your own personal Hell as you're reading these pages, and are screaming inside, "God, where are you? Doesn't anyone understand what I'm going through? God, I didn't think it was supposed to be like this? When is this madness going to stop?" Child of God, hold tight! He's heard your cry, and your answer is on the way.

Many years ago, one of these events happened to our family. It wasn't supposed to. Things like this don't happen to people like us. We were doing God's work! We were sacrificing our time, our family. We had given everything we had to God. He was not supposed to let anything bad happen to us. Yet in one single afternoon our world fell apart.

One Sunday afternoon, about fourteen years ago, we were enjoying a quiet time before church that evening. We had a couple from the church over. Our two younger children were playing outside, and our oldest son was spending the afternoon with a friend. It was about 3:30 p.m. when the phone rang. It was the family where our son was playing. The woman was crying uncontrollably and asked for my husband to come over immediately. We had no idea that our life was about to change forever.

The gentleman visiting that day went with my husband and his wife stayed with me. We heard nothing for the span of an hour-and-a-half. I was expecting to hear the phone ring when the car came screeching up to the house. At that point in time, a feeling of fear and helplessness came over me. I knew something was terribly wrong.

My husband opened the door and came in. By the look on his face, I knew something had happened to our son. But our son wasn't with him. WHAT WAS GOING ON? AND WHERE WAS MY SON?

As my husband told us the story, it felt like a bucket of ice cold water was being poured out over the top of me. I couldn't believe my ears. This was not supposed to happen! Not to my little boy! He was only eight years old!

Our son was playing with his friend, whose parents were in the military and lived on a military base. He and his friend were riding their bicycles as they always did. This day, though, someone decided to steal their childhood and innocence away from them. A six-foot-three, two hundred and thirty-pound nineteen-year-old male pushed the boys off their bikes, shoved them into the bushes and sexually molested them.

Thankfully the uncle of the boy our son was visiting felt something was wrong and ran to find the boys. He found them while the event was taking place. There was a fight between the two adults. Then the nineteen-year-old rode off on his bike, not to be found. Our son and his friend were bruised and scratched from the bushes, and they were scared to death. The boys were taken back to the house; and that is when we were called.

Now, remember, when my husband returned to the house, it was around 5:30 p.m. He had to get behind the pulpit and preach at 6:30 p.m. for the Sunday evening service. Yet the police, the MP's, and the military social services wanted to talk to one of the parents to fill out all the necessary reports. So I returned to the military base, with my son curled up in the floorboard of the back seat, to hear the whole story again.

Upon arrival at the military housing, I saw several police cars, military vehicles and people milling around everywhere. I walked in with my son and sat down, not knowing what I would see or hear.

It was true. The social workers had talked to the boys. Their stories matched, and the officers believed them. One lady came out to talk to me. Up until now, I thought I was doing pretty good, holding myself together. But what she said made me begin to shake from head to toe.

"Mrs. Fulton, we have determined that your son was sexually assaulted. He and his friend were questioned separately, and their stories are the same. We have also determined that your son was not penetrated." There it was! That word! "There was not enough time for penetration to take place." There it was again. That word! Quit saying that word! It's bad enough that this whole ordeal has taken place; but do you have to keep using that word on top of everything else? My son came out of the room where he was being questioned and walked over to me and said, "Mom, don't hate me! I'm sorry!" Hate you? You're sorry! At that point I think if the assailant had been in front of me, I would have killed him. How dare he do this to my child, my first born! I grabbed my son and held him as close as I could and prayed that this would not scar him nor turn his little heart away from God.

No one in the church knew what had happened that afternoon, only the couple that was staying with us that day. My husband preached that night, just like every other Sunday evening. But this night he came home and collapsed in a heap of tears and frustration because he was not able to fix this problem. Daddy's are always supposed to fix it; but this was one problem he couldn't fix. His son was broken now and he couldn't glue him back together.

The days that followed revealed many interesting facts. The assailant, three days before the incident with our son, had raped two little boys, ages two and three. Four days after the incident with our son, he raped a little girl, age five. Military police knew who he was and where he lived, yet seven days later had not arrested him. He had been seen at our son's school and was seen riding his bike all over the base. Something inside of me snapped. What was it going to take to get this guy off the streets?

I began making phone calls, asking questions, finding out information. Within two days I had found out the assailant's name, address, names of his parents, the names and addresses of the little boys he had raped and the name and address of the little girl he had raped. All of these events were taking place on a U.S. military base.

Here was my advantage. We were not military. We were civilian! So I called the General's office to talk to the General. Of course they wouldn't let me talk to the General himself, so one of his assistants talked to me. I told him about all the information I had acquired and his comment to me was, "Now Mrs. Fulton, you need to calm down." Calm down? You've got to be joking.

"I will not calm down," I told him. "I am not military. My husband is not military. We have no military privileges for you to take away from us. I've got nothing to lose when it comes to you. I will give you two days to remove this guy from the streets before I call the local T.V. station and make a full statement of what is going on there on post. I will also contact the radio station, along with the local newspaper. I will contact our Congressman, the mayor and the governor. Then I will come and plant myself on the General's desk until some kind of action is taken. Have I made myself clear?"

"Yes, ma'am!" Two days later he was off the streets and behind bars! Not until five months later did this case go to court.

That day at the courthouse, our case was in one room. The case with the little boys was in another room; and the case with the little girl was in another room still. We had to listen to the whole story again! Then we waited. One hour, two hours, three hours went by when finally the attorney came in with this statement. "They cleared the courtroom before they brought the accused in. He pleaded guilty to all charges. The judge would not allow any family members of the victims or the victims to be in the courtroom because he feared someone would try to kill the accused. The accused was being sent to a hospital for the criminally insane for three years. One year for each case. After that he would be evaluated to see what should be done with him next. His family was being removed from the base and all the military privileges were being stripped from them." Then he asked, did we have any questions?

As we walked out of that courtroom, the families of the little boys and the young girl walked out behind us. They were in tears consoling one another. These two families didn't have God to comfort them. I couldn't imagine going though such an event without the Lord helping us.

That day I realized that bad things do happen to good people; but I also realized that when those things happen, there is a God who will help you through the roughest times of your life. You know how I know that? Because it could have been worse. My son could have been penetrated! But he wasn't! God stopped it before it got to that point. Now my son is a handsome young man, married to his childhood sweetheart and they have a beautiful baby boy. Is God good? He sure is!

*****

"For God is not the author
of confusion but of peace...."
I Corinthians 13:33a
(TNKJV)

TEN

"I DON'T THINK SO!"

In our particular denomination during the time I was growing up, and also when we first entered into the ministry, pastors did not stay at one church very long. Eighteen months to two years was considered a long term pastorate. Thank God it's not that way now. Now you can, if the Lord allows, stay as long as you like.

Several times when I was a child and was not privy to knowledge of upcoming moves, I would hear we'd be moving from the pulpit when my father announced it to the congregation. I can't swear to it, but I'm sure that my mother was shocked a few times when she heard it too.

But never had I ever heard of a situation like the one my husband and I encountered while pastoring in the state of Louisiana. We felt that our time was up at this particular church. My husband put his name out for possible churches. We were asked to become a State and Christian Education Director. That meant we wouldn't be pastoring. We would be in a official state position in our denomination in the state of Hawaii. We were told to pack all our belongings, store the ones that we could not take (large pieces of furniture, etc.) and be ready to ship our car in three weeks.

We told our church we were leaving, read the letter of appointment of the incoming pastor. We packed up our things and stored our furniture. I was packed and ready to move with two days to spare. The church had a nice going-away for us and was preparing to receive their new pastor.

Thursday, before the Saturday when they were coming to move our things, we received a phone call. They told us that there was a snag in the plans. They asked could we hold off moving until they got back with us. A SNAG! What does that mean?

For us that meant that we had to sit in the

middle of all of our boxes with three babies, no toys to play with, no utensils to cook with and wait!

Thursday passed, no word. Friday passed, no word. Late Friday night a call come in. We're not going to Hawaii; but they think we'll be going to San Antonio, Texas. But wait, they said until they made sure. Saturday morning, a call. No San Antonio, TX, but they're pretty sure they want us in Virginia, but wait until they confirm. Saturday evening Virginia is out, but now Kansas is in. Again wait for further instructions.

Sunday, which was supposed to be our last Sunday, my husband preached. Following the service, we received another phone call. Kansas is out, San Antonio, TX is back in. This time they said this was for sure. Hello, I'd heard that before!!!!! Unlike the other times, we didn't hear back from them for more than two weeks.

The new pastor was en route to the church and we were unable to get in touch with him to tell him the status of what was going on. School was about to start for the new school year. The church was wondering what was going on. I was becoming very anxious and my husband was a nervous wreck.

Finally the phone call came. They want us to go to Michigan. MICHIGAN! I didn't feel God in that at all! NO, NOT AT ALL! I had not left my living room in the parsonage in Louisiana; and in the matter of two and a half weeks, my family was going to Hawaii, Texas, Virginia, Kansas, back to Texas and now MICHIGAN! I don't think so.

I told my husband, "Something is not right. There is far too much confusion in this move. And if I read my Bible correctly, CONFUSION IS NOT OF GOD!"

He agreed. Thank God. At this point, he called the brother in the Lord who was trying to place us and told him that we just didn't feel God in it for us to go to Michigan. Then is when I heard the statement that I will carry to my grave not understanding.

This individual said, "Just pack your U-Haul and your family and drive toward Cleveland, TN (that's where our church denomination headquarters is located). By the time you get here, we'll have you a church."

DO WHAT! Had everyone in the universe gone stark raving mad? What do you mean? Pack up and drive toward Cleveland?

My husband got off the phone and told me what was said to him. I probably would have laughed if I hadn't been so angry. I had no intentions of leaving my things in storage there in Louisiana, packing up all of my remaining earthly belongings, along with my children and dog, leave a church (that really didn't want us to go), leave a great parsonage and drive toward Cleveland. Well, not at least in this life time.

After a lengthy discussion, my husband called a gentleman who had always been very kind to us, someone in high authority in our denomination. He told him of our plight, and requested his very much needed advice. Thank God some leaders still listen to the voice of God.

He told my husband, "Do not pack up and drive toward Cleveland. Give me some time and I'll work something out for you." That was all we needed.

Sunday morning my husband got up to preach and unresigned the church, read the letter of appointment, appointing himself back as pastor of the church. The incoming pastor was located and the church leadership (in Cleveland) sent him to Virginia. I put my kids in school; and for the next three months we pastored that church again.

Did I unpack? Certainly not! Someone was working something out for us. In November we received a call that sent us to a church in New York. This is were we experienced one of the greatest moves of God in our ministry, up until that time.

If that's the way my parents were treated, thank God I only heard from the pulpit that it was time to move. It was hard enough moving. I would have been a nervous wreck as a child if I had to deal with the rest of all the mess.

But in our waiting and submitting to the authority over us in the Lord, the Lord prepared the way for us to have a successful ministry in New York. If we had gone to any of the other places, that move of God that we experienced in New York, might not have happened and my son would not have met his wife-to-be.

So if you don't understand what's going on in your life, hang on! God is more than likely preparing the way for you to have one of the greatest moves of God in your life that you've ever experienced.

"I Don't Think So!"

*****

"Behold, how good and how pleasant it is for brethren to dwell together in unity!"
Psalm 133:1
(TAB)

ELEVEN

"FUN TIME...CHURCH DISPUTES"

*C*hurch disputes are always a fun time in the life of the pastor and his family. It's almost as if people think we wear a flashing neon sign on our heads that says, "Hurt us, we love it. That's what we're here for. We don't have feelings. We love being abused."

When dealing with church disputes, especially when writing about them, I would run out of ink and paper if I tried to mention them all. If you just look at the negative and the hurt, it would be easy to hang up the ministry on a rusty nail and turn around and walk away. But if you can grow and learn and try to see where God is taking you, these experiences can be very valuable. Of course it may not feel like it while you are going through the event.

When my husband and I first started out in the ministry, our biggest disputes were whether women could wear pants, make-up and jewelry or cut their hair. Thank God He started us off with the foolish little disputes.

I know the Bible says that women shouldn't wear men's clothing. As far as I know, to this day I haven't worn a pair of men's pants. They've all been women's pants, thank you! And if you want to get technical, everyone in Bible times wore robes or something to that effect (men and women alike). The only difference was the type of material used in men and women's garments. Women were not allowed to wear the materials used in men's garments.

And if we can't wear make-up, then I guess Queen Esther wouldn't be welcome in most of our churches. The Bible says she was prepared for the King. Her clothes were just right. Her face was just right. Her hair was just right. She was taught how to walk properly. She was taught how to talk properly. She was drenched in perfumes. Thank God the church has changed some in these areas. I remember when women had to walk into church looking like an unmade bed and had a face looking like a whitewashed barn. While this was considered to be holy, these same women's husbands were complimenting other women who were wearing a little make-up and had their hair styled. Sound familiar?

Now as we increased in experience in the ministry, disputes also increased in intensity. We went from clothing and hair to "You're in my seat. I've sat there for the past fifty years."

We were coming back from England, where we pastored a military church, and we were taking a small church in the state of Mississippi. The only information that we knew about this church was that there had been no one saved in the past twenty-two years and that it was a family church. What harm could there be here? They weren't doing anything or going anywhere!

Our first Sunday we gathered up our little family, which consisted of my husband, me and our two small boys, ages two and a half years and six weeks. After entering the church, I scoped out the sanctuary for a place to sit with the boys and all the items needed to keep a two and a half year old boy occupied and everything that a six week old would need, which included the baby's carrying seat and diaper bag. I saw that there were three sections. Each section had about seven rows of pews. This should be easy enough. Wrong answer!

My first choice was the right section about row five. Seemed safe enough. Boys in place, items arranged for the boys during service. When I felt someone standing behind me. As I turned around, an older man and woman told me I was sitting in their seat. I apologized, gathered my things, and took the boys to another seat on the left side about row six. No sooner had I gotten seated when a man came and told me I was in his seat. Again I gathered the boys' items and the boys and found a seat on the right side, last row. Again I was told I was in someone's seat and again I moved. This time I didn't take a seat anywhere. I waited until service began and everyone had arrived and was seated. To my amazement I discovered something very interesting. Do you remember how I said this was a family church? Well, no one was sitting in the middle section. Why?

One family was on the right side and the other family was on the left side. The two families hated one another, kind of like the Hatfield and the McCoy's. The two sides did not talk to one other, or even acknowledge each other's presence.

Even when they went to the choir, they entered from opposite sides of the platform and sat on opposite sides of the choir loft, leaving the same way they had arrived.

After observing this from the back of the church with the boys, I decided it was safe to sit in the middle section. It seemed to be the neutral zone. There I sat with my boys for the long six months we were at that church.

To quote the 86-year-old mother of the church during one meeting just before we left, "We've seen pastors come, and we've seen them go, and we're still here." That's right, you've seen them come and you've seen them go and you're still sitting in that same old seat.

Sad isn't it, when Christians are more concerned about where they sit in church than what's being done for God? Think about it. How many churches do you know that are still like that today?

As time went by, we became more mature in ministry and the disputes also became more mature in nature.

How about this one for being mature? We pastored one church in Louisiana for about six weeks, which seemed like sixty years. They had a brand spanking new sanctuary. There were no Sunday School rooms. There was no fellowship hall and no offices. There were two bathrooms, a nursery (with one small crib) and the sanctuary.

The problem started when we arrived on the scene with three children. Apparently, children were not a part of the over-all plan for this church. After that, things just seemed to get worse. In this newly-built sanctuary there were beautiful padded pews, a new organ and a $20,000 baby grand piano. There was no altar. Instead, six steps leading to the platform were padded which you could use for an altar and prayer.

Upon our arrival, there was no pianist. Being that I could play, I marched myself up and sat down for worship service. I was promptly told that the piano was just for show and no one, including myself, was to touch it. They would sing with tapes. This was the same policy for the organ.

No live music, no Sunday School, no altar. Do you understand now why we only stayed six weeks? I don't believe Jesus Christ himself would have been welcome there. Ultimately the church closed its doors and was sold. Isn't it great to be so mature and spiritual that children are not even welcome in your church? If I'm not mistaken, Jesus said, "Forbid them not to come unto me."

The two greatest disputes possible in the church today is probably tithes & offerings and, of course, that special day that we honor and appreciate the Pastor and his family.

When it comes to money, people especially church folks, really have a problem with it. I've heard statements, and you have too, like "that's all they're after is our money." Or "That's all they ever talk about is money." Or "I can't afford to pay my tithes, and now they want an offering." Or "Tithing is an Old Testament principle. We're under grace now. Jesus came to abolish the old law." Or "I pay my tithes and give in the offering; now I want to know exactly how and where it's spent." Or "If it's not done this way, I'll withhold my tithes."

The excuses for not giving could fill a book, and not one would be valid. The Bible says to pay ten percent of your increase. Got a problem with that? Talk to God about it. He wrote the Book and trust me, you're not so special that He is going to change it after all this time just for you. And He didn't say, "Give your tithes to the youth pastor or to your neighbor." He said, "Bring your tithes into the storehouse (church) that there may be meat at my table." If you want to give the youth pastor or your neighbor something, give them an offering that's above your tithes.

And God forbid, never take up more than one offering in church. You may have half your congregation get up and walk out. How dare you?

I remember one such time when we had a guest speaker. There were about one hundred and seventy-five people in service that night when my husband took up the evening offering, which was to go to the speaker. A grand total of $34 and change came in. So before the speaker got up to speak, my husband returned to the pulpit and received another offering. As soon as he mentioned a second offering, three ladies jumped up and ran out of the building holding their heads and crying at the top of their lungs.

It took about five minutes to receive the second offering and turn the service over to the speaker, at which time my husband followed the ladies out of the church. What he found was a sight for sure.

Two of the ladies were standing out in the parking lot crying and praying loud enough to bring down the walls of Jericho. The third lady was lying on the ground crying hysterically. One of the standing ladies approached my husband and told him that the one on the ground didn't have money to put in the second offering and was made to feel that she wasn't worthy to be in service. She then proceeded to tell my husband that because he had received a second offering, he was not a man of God. She continued, "Before the sun sets tomorrow, you will become sick and die." That was twelve years ago and he's still kicking!

Listen, it doesn't matter if one or a hundred

and one offerings are taken during a service, give in the offering God tells you to give in. In our church in Miami, my husband might take one, maybe two, quite often three offerings. Once I even saw him take up five offerings. That's crazy you say, but if you're one of the late arriving members that slip in just after the offering, God wants you to be able to give also and be blessed. And for those who arrive at the altar service, you need to receive your blessing too, which comes from giving.

Now what about the day that is set aside to honor and appreciate the pastor and his family? Respectfully speaking, I refer to it as <u>"The Day from Hell!"</u> And according to just about every pastor and his family that I have talked to, they feel the same way. Why not call it "Give the pastor a break down day." Or, "Let's see how much stress one person can take day." Or, "Let's see how many people will get upset and leave the church day."

There was a lady in one church that we pastored who wanted to do a whole week for us, maybe even two weeks. I thought I was going to faint. I can't imagine a week and certainly not two weeks. If that ever happens, please just medicate me and wake me when it's over.

It seems like it should be such a harmless day. The Bible says to give honor where honor is due. I think giving your whole life to the church and to others should require one day out of the year for the church members to be kind to you. After all, it's only one day!

Needless to say, Pastor Appreciation Day is not my most favorite day of the year. It's too bad, too. We have Secretary's Day, Grandparents' Day, Mother's Day, Father's Day, President's Day, Flag Day, Boss' Day, and even Groundhog Day. We celebrate leprechauns and cupid's. We celebrate the first day of the year. We celebrate veterans and even those who have passed on with Memorial Day. But God help us on that one day of the year when we appreciate the man and his family who have been there in every crisis of your life, the one who has made sure you get the Word of God week in and week out, the one who was there when you birthed your babies or laid a loved one to rest.

Unless you are in the ministry, you may not and probably won't understand this, but God doesn't require the sheep to leave parents, brothers and sisters, aunts and uncles, nieces and nephews for years at a time, ultimately leaving children in various parts of the states or the world to go and do the work of the Lord. The sheep aren't required to do so; but the shepherds are. That's the difference between the sheep and the shepherd. The shepherd is willing to do so. If for no other reason, honor and appreciate them for that. It's a sacrifice the sheep will never know or understand.

So from me to all the pastors, pastors' wives and all of their children, 'HAPPY PASTOR APPRE-CIATION DAY!' You are all special and are worth all the honor you can get. Take all the good that comes your way and throw all the rest out with all those who are upset and walk out. Trust me, you are better off without them. They are only a hin-drance to your ministry.

*****

"And Delilah said to Samson, Tell me, I pray you, wherein your great strength lies, and with what you might be bound to sub- due you."

Judges 16:6

(TAB)

TWELVE

"THE OTHER WOMAN"

Once an older sister in the Lord shared with me that there will always be, let's refer to her as "the other woman" in the church who will somehow mysteriously find out the things that the pastor likes, or at least what she thinks he likes and make sure he gets them.

Now let me make this very clear. This "other woman" comes in every size and shape imaginable. Her financial status, racial background and education makes no difference. Her hair may be black, brown, blonde. With the colors people wear today, it could even be green. They can come from the "old school" and wear no make-up or jewelry or they can come from the "I'm out of bondage group" with make-up and whatever feels good. She can be married or single, it makes no difference. But be assured, she is in every church.

Now after more than twenty years in the ministry, they are easy to spot coming. They might as well wear a big red ribbon in their hair or paint big yellow spots all over their face to announce their arrival. My question is, after all these years, why is it still hard for pastors to see them?

The good ones try to sneak up on you, while there are some who are not quite so tactful. So this chapter we devote to "the other woman," as no ministry would be complete without them.

While reading this chapter, you may come up with several names for "the other woman" who has attached herself to your husband. How do I know? Because the list is endless; so I'm just going to mention a few.

Let's begin with the "Time Monopolizing Woman." We all know this woman, the one who can't seem to make a decision without calling the pastor. The phone starts ringing at 6 a.m. She wants to know if it's possible to come by the house or the office to discuss something going on in the church or in her life. She doesn't want counsel. She just wants to talk. After all, isn't that what the pastor is for, to be at her beckon call? Not only is she the first to call in the morning, but usually the last to call at night. Thank God for caller I.D. Now when "Sister Time Monopolizer" calls, the pastor doesn't have to pick up. Now ladies, don't you wish he'd do that with some of those men members?

Next let's discuss the "Always Needing Counseling Woman." "Help me pastor, my husband doesn't treat me right." "Oh pastor, my kids are so unruly." "Pastor, I can't seem to get out of this depression." "Pastor, what should I do? My job is so stressful." "Pastor, I don't feel like I'm liked in the church." "Pastor, I'm not getting fed during the services." "Pastor, we never have enough money." "Pastor, Pastor, Pastor!"

I'm not referring to a dozen women each with a single complaint. I am referring to "ONE" woman. And it's not the pastor's wife. There have been a few times I felt like calling the office and setting up an appointment with my husband for counseling, just so I could see him. And at one time or the other I probably have had one or all of these complaints. But by the time my husband comes home from the office, he doesn't feel like hearing any complaints from me, because "Sister Always

Needing Counseling" has filled his head with so much garbage that if he hears one more complaint he will erupt like a volcano.

Moving on to one of my favorite sisters. Let's call her the "I Want To Be Your Friend Woman." Hello! If he needed another woman friend God wouldn't have given him a WIFE!

Yet this woman will do everything she can to befriend the pastor, from calling to just check on his day (but not yours), or sending a card to encourage him (not the two of you). She will always compliment his clothing and of course his preaching. And a dead give away, she will always laugh at his jokes.

These women are usually not too subtle, at least not to the eyes of the pastor's wife. Usually "Sister, I Want To Be The Pastor's Friend" will eliminate the pastor's wife from all conversations. The one thing that can't be missed is her body language...the way she walks, her posture while she's around him, eye glances. Ministers, please open your eyes. Your wives are not just being critical or jealous of this woman. Your wife is looking out for your ministry and soul. This "I Want To Be Your Friend Woman" is a true threat to your ministry. She may come in appearing to be a friend, but tell me if I'm wrong, don't wolves come in wearing sheep's clothing seeking a sheep to destroy?

One of the easiest detectable women of the church is the "Gift Bearing Woman." You know this woman. She knows the pastor's birthday and anniversary. She'll get him a Christmas gift, Thanksgiving gift, New Years gift, you name it. No holiday or special day will go without some sort of present. Cards come weekly in the mail.

In one church we pastored, this one "Gift Bearing Woman" decided that the Pastor should be dressed in western clothes. So each week she bought him a different piece of clothing. First came the shirt complete with the western fringe. Next came a pair of tight fitting jeans. Of course no self respecting cowboy would be seen without his hat, boots and belt. If she'd only have given him a gun & holster, I could have shot her with it. Of course that wouldn't have been too spiritual. But I know I would have felt better.

I often wondered, "Did it ever occur to her to buy me or any of the children gifts?" Well, it didn't to this woman (or any other "Gift Bearing Woman" that I've met or heard about). Not that I ever wanted a gift, but it would have been nice to be included. She could have at least bought me the spurs!

After this next woman, nothing ever shocked me again. Let's call her, "The I'm An Asset To Your Ministry Woman." I could call her something else, but I'll stick with that name for the time being.

There have been a few times in our ministry that these women have risen their heads. The first time we were very young in the ministry; and to be truthful with you, I didn't know this type of woman existed. Our adult Sunday School teacher, who was married and had children, thought she was one of the more spiritual people in the church. She was very outgoing and very demonstrative in her personality, while I was more on the quiet side. There came a time when she and her husband were having some problems so she threw herself into her studies and teachings, in her eyes making her only more spiritual than anyone in the church. Sometime during her studies and prayer time, she felt God telling her to tell me that she had more to offer my husband's ministry than I did and that I would be more suited to be with her husband. Oh Really!

So after one of her prayer times with God, you know, she came and shared her new found revelation with me. Since we were still very new in the ministry, I hadn't developed all the spiritual tactfulness that comes with time. I promptly began to laugh hysterically. Through my tears I glanced up at this woman who didn't see anything funny about the situation. I said, "You're joking, right? You can't be serious!" To which she replied, "No." I straightened up and looked her square in the eyes and said, "Honey, without me he has no ministry; and even if you got him, after a week you'd be begging me to take him back. Now get out of my house."

She was my first experience with "STUPIDITY" but not my last. What is it with women who feel they have a talent that is associated with ministry? Teaching, preaching, music, etc. One woman was a piano player, and she felt she was a good singer also. She was in her second marriage and wanted terribly to be in full-time ministry. That would have been all right, but she wanted that full-time ministry with my husband. Don't figure, it wasn't like my husband needed a second full-time partner in ministry.

Anyway, one evening during the altar call, she motioned to me to come to the piano. I thought she might want to go to the altar to pray or be prayed for. Or maybe she needed a break from playing for a while. Whichever, I went and sat next to her at the piano. She continued playing and leaned over to me and whispered, "If you would get out of the way, your husband and I would have a great ministry together."

I looked up into the face of a dead serious woman. So I asked, "What about your husband?" She replied, "He's not interested in ministry." I said, "Too bad, but my husband already has a wife, ministry partner and a piano player, ME. And I'm sure he isn't interested in anything that you have to offer him, ministry wise, talent wise or any other wise." I went home and shared with my husband that he was a wanted man. If you've ever seen someone seasick, you know that lovely green color, that "I'm going to lose my lunch" color. that was him. Just the thought of this woman made him sick. So now when he gets on my nerves, I offer to give her a call to see if I can still take her up on her offer. That usually settles him right down.

I want to talk about one more woman. How about this one, the "Let's Be Prayer Partners Woman"? What could be the harm in praying? Just think about it. Prayer can be, and usually is, one of the most personal and private times of ones life. It's where you empty your heart and dreams and visions out to the Lord. It's where you give God your hurts and struggles. It's where you pray for people you love or people you have problems with. It's where you pray for your church and it's members and situations affecting the membership of the church. Prayer is also where you rejoice over answered prayers, where you tell God all your victories. People are drawn together by prayer. Relationships are developed through prayer. Trusts are formed through prayer. Hearts touch through prayer. Do you see the danger of a woman being the pastor's prayer partner?

Pastor, evangelist, ministers, if you need a prayer partner, pray with your wife or gather brothers in the Lord around you who are of like vision and spirit and pray. Don't be so naive or innocent to think that because it's just prayer that nothing will happen. I've seen it happen too many times, where a Man of God has a woman prayer partner or a woman intercessor, a bond and closeness develops. Before you know it, a man's ministry is destroyed, along with his marriage.

Just a note to close out this chapter. Ladies, "The Other Woman" will always be with us, and that's a fact. But you need to realize something. It's just like a woman who falls in love with her OB/GYN doctor. The doctor makes her feel good about herself and encourages her when she feels like a blimp. It's not the man, but the caring, the attention that she has fallen for. So it is with your husband. It's not really him she wants. It's what he offers -- a kind word, a gentle prayer, a caring attitude (that's for those who are lonely). For the blatant, "I want your husband woman," it's still not him they want. It's the position he holds, not the man. I share that with my husband all the time. "Dear, they really don't want you. It's the position of pastor. If they had you, they wouldn't know what to do with you. It's better you just stay with me. I already

know how strange you are and I love you anyway."
This always brings things into perspective a little.

"The Other Woman"

*****

"Flee also youthful lusts:
but follow righteousness,
faith, charity, peace, with
them that call on the Lord
out of a pure heart."
II Timothy 2:22
(KJ)

THIRTEEN

"THE OTHER MAN"

believe that it's only fair that if I devote a full chapter to "The Other Woman" in the church that I also devote a chapter to "The Other Man" in the church. He is just as damaging to the ministry as "The Other Woman".

We had a learned minister come hold a series of meetings for us several years ago. One of the topics he wanted to discuss was marriage and relationships between men and women in the church. We took him to dinner. While eating, he shared with us an overall outline of what this class would consist of. Much of what he said was excellent information which I had thought for years should be taught in the church. I was listening intently when he made a statement that about blew me off my chair.

This is the statement. "It has been common knowledge in the church world that some men in ministry have had extramarital affairs. After getting caught, they are given a slap on the hand by the officials of the church, and then moved to another church or even promoted. All this is common knowledge. But the one thing that is becoming more and more common is that ministers' wives are now having affairs. I don't understand what could be causing this rise of events. I wish someone could explain it to me."

That last sentence was enough to get a quick, unrehearsed response from me. In fact, I jumped on that statement with a vengeance. I came across so strongly that my husband didn't know how to respond or even how to continue the conversation when I was finished.

"What don't you understand? Don't you understand that women whose husbands are in the ministry are tired of coming second to the ministry? Or don't you understand that they are tired of coming second to every member in the church? It just might be that they are tired of all the kind words in his vocabulary going to everyone else, when the wife might need a kind word? Maybe it's that there aren't enough hours in the day for all the church events throughout the week plus her and the children! Could it be that most ministers and pastors never take a day off? Maybe it's because most ministers' wives feel more like a business partner than a wife? Why would it shock you that the women are going out and having affairs? Why would it shock you that at the first kind word given to her that she wouldn't jump on it? Why would it shock you that when someone gives her a little attention or compliments her, that she wouldn't follow him to the ends of the earth? I can assure you that most women don't feel like vacation time is going to listen to her husband preach a revival. Or that the definition of "time alone" is not when he goes to preach a revival and leaves her alone with the kids for a week. I don't know why you don't understand it. I understand it completely. I'm just surprised that according to your statistics that it's not more women than men who are having affairs."

At that moment you could hear a pin drop. For the rest of dinner, it was general chit-chat.

Another time I was at a ministers' wives conference. One of the guest speakers spoke on "what to do when Saul comes calling." There were approximately 600 women there that day. As the speaker spoke, an eerie hush fell over the room. It was as if every lady in that room could relate with what she was talking about.

She told a story about a young couple that she had met when she had first come to the United States. (She was from England). This couple had been high school sweethearts. They had been in love since the end of elementary school. After graduating from high school, they immediately got married and went into ministry as youth pastors of their local church. They had been married less than a year when the speaker first met them.

Our speaker asked the young lady how things were going and was she happy in the ministry. Here is the young lady's response. "I am so happy. I love being married. I love being in the ministry. There is nothing that could happen that could come between my husband and me. We are so much in love. He is my David." (Referring to David in the Bible, who was described as being of a ruddy countance.) At that time the speaker said, "So you've never met Saul then?" (Referring to Saul in the Bible who was described as being tall and handsome and having a way with words.) "No," the young lady replied.

"Be careful," our speaker told the young lady. "For every David, there will be a Saul who will come calling." At that point their conversation was over.

Nearly a year later our speaker said that she returned to that same church to hold another series of meetings. A young girl came up to her, haggard looking, bags under her eyes, clothes tattered and very unsure of her speech. The young girl asked if the speaker remembered her. Our speaker said she look long and hard at the girl and could not recognize her. She said, "No, I'm sorry. I don't recall who you are."

"I'm the girl that you told about a year ago to look out for Saul, because he would come calling."

"Oh yes. How have you been?"

"Not good."

"Why?"

"Saul came calling!"

The youth pastor and his wife were now divorced. During that first year, she felt neglected. Someone came by her way and paid her a little attention. Be assured that if the devil has someone to pull the pastor down, he will also have someone just as appealing to pull the pastor's wife down.

Let me share one more story before I close out this chapter. While we were pastoring in New York, an event took place that rattled me to my bones.

We were pastoring a church where the Lord

had truly blessed us. It was growing in numbers, finances, but most important it was growing spiritually. We had something happening every night of the week. We had programs for every imaginable situation that could arise in your life.

During this time we had become friends with a neighboring pastor and his wife. Their church was about 45 minutes from ours. So most of our times spent together were at camp meetings, prayer conferences or other meetings that might bring all the churches in the area together.

One day during a ministers' meeting, my husband was sitting next to, let's call him John Doe. Why John Doe, you ask? Because most "John Doe's" in the secular society get lost in the system, and so do a lot of couples get lost in the church system. This couple being one of them.

As they were sitting there, the speaker was talking about the upcoming singles' retreat. John leaned over to my husband and said, "I'll more than likely be at that retreat."

My husband jokingly said, "Me, too." But when he turned to see John's expression to his little joke, John wasn't smiling or laughing. My husband asked him what the problem was. John began telling a story that unfolded like many others that I have heard over the past several years.

There was a family in his church whose oldest son had become very sick and died. If that wasn't bad enough, the next son also became sick with the same disease. He also died. This family's youngest son was the youth pastor of the church and dating the pastor's daughter. After his brothers' deaths the youth pastor went into a deep depression, not knowing if he could possibly be next.

During this time the pastor's wife felt so badly for the young man. What started out as the love of a mother and pastor's wife for a grieving boy turned into something more. After several weeks of counseling one on one with him, her feelings for him became very strong. Her feelings were so strong that it didn't matter any longer that this wasn't her husband, so strong that it didn't matter any longer that this was her daughter's boyfriend, so strong that it didn't matter that it was the youth pastor of her husbands' church, so strong that it lead them into an affair that lasted for several months before anyone found out.

Why did it affect me so hard? Where was I? Why wasn't I there for her? How could I have been so busy that I couldn't have seen the signs of what was coming? More important, if it hadn't been for the grace of God, it could have been me. This was my friend! Why her and not me?

So ladies, while you are keeping an eye out

for "The Other Woman," be sure not to let your guards down so the "The Other Man" slips in unnoticed. None of us are exempt from the tricks of the devil.

To end this, let me give you something to think about. Can you be so busy in your own church, your own world, that you miss out on the friends God has placed in your life? Are your sheep so important, that you miss the signs in "the shepherds" that you see so quickly in the sheep? Are you so intimidated by other ministers that you don't reach out when they need help? Are you so afraid that if they find out you are human and hurt, too, that your secrets will get out?

We need to check our priorities and see what is really important. Is it so impossible to be a shepherd to the sheep as well as to be there for our peers (other ministers and their families) as well as to take care of our own families?

If God Almighty has called you to do His bidding, then He will give you the knowledge and the strength and the ability to do all three.

"The Other Man"

*****

"Create in me a clean heart, O God, And renew a steadfast spirit within me."
Psalms 51:10
(TNKJV)

FOURTEEN

"THE CHURCH FROM HELL"

*Y*ou had better be careful what you ask God for, because if you ask Him enough, you just may get it. Even if it isn't something you need! "Won't happen, can't happen," you say. God wouldn't give you something that wasn't good for you. God wouldn't give you something or let you go through something if He knew you might get wounded or hurt through the event. Really?

Let's ask the children of Israel who begged and begged for a King. "We want a King! We want a King! All the other nations have a King and we want one too." Up until that time, they were led by the Man of God. But no, they wanted a king. God told them through His prophet that they did not need a King, but they persisted. They wanted a King. So God gave them a King. After God gave them the King that they prayed and pleaded for, they didn't know what to do with him. So be careful what you pray for. You just may end up with what you've asked for; and after you get it, nine times out of ten you'll realize, you really don't want it or need it.

If God says, if you do things my way, this will be the end results. Do it! If you don't, you may go around the bush a few times, when just one trip around the bush wouldn't even have been necessary if you had done it God's way.

So began our trip, over an answered prayer that we really didn't want (but didn't know at the time). This experience to an answered prayer, I lovingly call my experience at "The Church From Hell." This experience had nothing to do with the church or it's members itself, but more to do with the condition of my heart and my family at that present time.

Just a note here, if every church you pastor is "the church from hell," I'd venture to say, you are in the wrong business. No church is without it's problems; but if every church you choose is wrong, you had better reassess your calling. That's not what I'm referring to here. What I'm referring to is here is the possibility of over the course of twenty or thirty years there will likely be one, possible two churches, that you would like to wipe out of your memory completely. Total amnesia! Complete blackout! As if it never happened! Get my drift? For me, while at this church, events took place in my heart and life that I would rather forget.

From the day that I married my husband, I have heard him say, "I really want to pastor in my home state." God only knows how many times I had heard that statement. But we were young. I thought it would pass. I prayed it would pass; and he prayed it would come to pass. Guess whose prayers won out?

We were pastoring a strong, progressive church. The Lord had blessed us with a very successful ministry. After about four years, which for us was a long time in one place, my husband overheard a conversation by the elders of the church that wounded his spirit. In his wounded condition, he received a call, out of the blue, about changing churches with a man from, you guessed it, my husband's home state. I couldn't believe it. What was going on? You can't make decisions when you are emotionally upset!

My feelings were, this couldn't possibly be from God. My husband's feelings were, "This had to be from God." How could things get so confusing in the span of three days? Conversation overheard on Saturday, crushed and wounded spirit all day Sunday, phone call on Monday! But what was ahead became a nightmare. All I wanted to do was wake up and have things as they were before that dreaded overheard conversation. Life has not been the same since.

As you may have guessed, we took the church. It was a decision that I let my husband make totally on his own. I felt that if I gave my opinion, and he chose not to go, that somewhere down the road, he'd say, "I had an opportunity to pastor the largest church in my home state, and you didn't want to go." Or if I said "O.K. let's go", and it didn't work he'd say, "If you had told me you didn't want to go, we wouldn't be in this mess now." Any way I looked at it, somehow I'd get blamed. Now I know none of you have ever felt that way, but that's how I felt. I felt I was in a no-win situation.

The day my husband preached his farewell sermon, someone from the congregation snuck into his office and took our van keys and started waving them at him during the sermon. Also during the sermon, no less, this individual shouted out, "I've got your keys, you aren't going anywhere."

The keys then were passed around the church. Needless to say, the farewell sermon turned into a game of hide-and-seek trying to find the van keys.

After the service, it was time for the closing prayer. My husband asked one of the men to come and close in prayer. He also told the church that during the prayer that he and his family would slip out and leave. It was hard enough to leave, so let there be as few tears as possible. Good plan, only if it had worked!

While we were trying to "SLIP OUT," so did the majority of the congregation. I felt like a rock star having pieces of my clothing ripped off. People were touching our hair. They were all trying to hug us. Just as I stepped out the front door, I turned and saw the youth of the church hanging all over our boys screaming, "Don't take them! We love you! Please don't go!"

There were about twenty-five steps down to the parking lot. The steps were lined with people. Grabbing, touching, giving gifts and cards. I didn't know if we would make it to the van. Yet when we finally got to the van, there was no possible way of getting into it. Even though we had retrieved the keys, the van was packed full of presents, gifts, balloons, food, picnic baskets, candy, books, magazines, flowers. Not only was it packed full, the outside was covered with shaving cream, stickers, balloons and on the door handles was Vaseline.

They were saying, "Go if you must, but we're not going to make this easy on you." When we finally pulled out of the parking lot, I began crying -- and I continued crying for the next fourteen months.

I have followed my husband around the world. I have toted my children from coast to coast and beyond. I have lived in trailers and in apartments above Sunday School rooms. I've lived in the jungle and in the swamp. I delivered my first child in a Spanish hospital in the middle of the jungle with nurses and doctors who spoke only Spanish. I delivered my second child in a large hospital in England. During delivery, there were seventeen student nurses observing natural childbirth. I could, with the best of them, turn on feelings for the people of the church we were pastoring. But as soon as we were gone, they were "Out Of Sight, Out Of Mind." NO PROBLEM! The only problem was, that now I was tired of playing the game. I somehow adjusted to all the other moves, but this one I didn't. I couldn't. I was tired. My heart hurt. I missed my friends. I didn't want to move. I didn't want to live in another place. But I knew the game. I knew what I was supposed to do.

We took our time in getting to the new

church. It took us about five days to get there. We met the welcoming committee at the church. Everything was going as it always did at a new church. First they wanted us to view the church. Great! The minute I walked into the sanctuary, I became sick to my stomach. Call it nerves; call it emotions; call it spiritual; call it what you will; but for the next fourteen months, I vomited every day. Literally. That was the easy part of it.

No sooner had we gotten into the house, the phone started ringing. It was people from our former church. They were begging us to come back. For the next six months, we received hundreds of calls a week asking for direction in their lives, wanting to know when we were coming back, asking if the new pastor was doing the right things.

This alone would have been stressful enough, yet tension and frustration in my life just seemed to continue to build. The people at our new church also needed a pastor. They also were hurting and needed direction in their lives. They truly wanted a move of God, and they believed we could bring that to their church and their community. Even if that was all, I could have worked through my feelings and tried to adjust and move on. But the plot thickens.

My children were very unhappy. My boys were young teenagers. They missed their friends, their school and their youth group. In the middle of our first service at our new church, our oldest son jumped up and screamed, "I hate it here; I want to go home." He ran out of the church crying. My heart sank even lower than it already was.

On top of all of this, during our entire ministry and marriage, we had never lived close to either of our families. Our only time with our families were at Christmas and sometimes in the summers. That is if we had enough money to get home. But now, being in my husband's home state, and being that I am from the adjoining state, we were close enough to our families that we were faced with not only church issues but family issues.

It's one thing to confront the demons from someone else's past, but it's another thing altogether to confront the demons of your own past. Every family has skeletons. But give me a break, did they all have to surface now?

So here was our dilemma. Our former church was looking for answers. Our new church was looking for answers. My kids were looking for answers. Our families were looking for answers. What was the common link between all of these? Me and my husband!

The more we struggled for answers, the deeper the depression became. So much so that we both ended up in counseling. No one knew.

They were all concerned about receiving their own answers. What we were going through came second to everyone else. I had been saved long enough to know it wasn't my responsibility to have the answer for everyone. Yet church members, family members, and the children needed answers. And they needed them now!

If all of this wasn't stressful enough, I became sick. What was wrong with me? After nine months of tests and treatments, the doctor said, "Mrs. Fulton, you are going to have to get rid of some stress in your life." O.K. Where should I begin? The church? Our kids? Our families? The place we were living? Our marriage? Our ministry? Which one should go first?

Stress wasn't the problem. Stress was only a symptom of the problem. My problem was that I was unhappy and angry at my husband for moving me and the kids away from a place that I loved. Instead of dealing with all that misery, I turned it inside and it affected my physical body. During nine months of doctors' and hospital calls, scans and probes, pills and shots, they determined it was stress. I ended up on twenty-seven prescription drugs and still they couldn't find a physical problem. That's because anger and bitterness will kill you. That was what was happening to me. I didn't want to be in the ministry any more. I didn't want to be married any more. I didn't want to be responsible for anything or anyone again. STOP THE WORLD AND LET ME OFF, NOW!

The one thing that I valued most, my sanity, was being stripped away; and I didn't know how to stop it. How could this be happening? I had always believed that Christians with emotional or mental problems just needed to grow up and stop acting like babies. Now I had become that person that I had no tolerance for. Was this a cruel joke from God? This couldn't possibly be my fault.

Saint of God, anger and bitterness will drive you into a deep, dark pit and you won't know how you got there and you won't know how to get out. I prayed every day. I read my Bible every day. I'd play gospel music and listen to TBN every night. I went through all the motions in church, yet felt nothing inside. Then I got to the place in my life when I prayed for God to kill me.

I remember the very day I prayed that prayer. I was sick, very sick. I had been vomiting all week. I had a constant headache. After all these years of me never being sick, my husband didn't know what to do with me. So he didn't do anything except get mad at me for being sick. The sicker I got, the madder he got. Why was he mad at me? This was all his fault to begin with. But as I laid on the bathroom floor, an elderly lady about 87 years old, built like a brick wall, marched herself into my house, up the stairs and entered my bathroom unannounced. She sat down beside me on the floor. she picked me up like a little baby and started rocking me back and forth saying, "You will not die. You will live. You will not die. You will live."

Who told her what I had just prayed? Who asked her to come and pray for me? Why was she speaking life into me when all I wanted to do was die? That was the first time she had done that, but not the last. She marched herself into our home several times and picked me up like a rag doll and said, "You will not die. You will live." To this sainted sister in the Lord, I will always be grateful. God had a plan bigger than me, and I needed to get myself out of the way. I needed to repent of anger and bitterness and ask God to forgive me, as well as all those I had offended in the middle of my sin.

Did we fix all the problems in that church? Of course not! They've been through several pastors since we were there and still the problem remains. Did we fix all of our families problems? Not hardly! In fact we probably left more than were originally there when we arrived. Did we answer all the questions from our former church? No! No! No!

So how about us? We took a church in another state across country and moved our family one more time. Were all our problems over? No, but I can assure you of one thing. The message we preached before, the lesson we taught before our experience at the "church from hell", was now being preached and being taught from a broken and contrite spirit. The Lord had taken us through a breaking process, and had sewn us back together like only He can do. The songs I sang before took on new meaning because I no longer depended on my own talent, but only on what He allowed me to have. Now I understand that I am nothing without Jesus Christ.

During the entire fourteen months that we were going through our journey of brokenness, I read the same scripture everyday. That scripture was Psalms 51. Don't be so stubborn that it takes you fourteen months of hell before you allow God to "renew a right spirit in you."

"The Church From Hell"

145

*****

"For you fashioned my inmost being, you knit me together in my mother's womb. I thank you because I am awesomely made, wonderfully; your works are wonders - I know this very well. My bones were not hidden from you when I was being made in secret, intricately woven in the depths of the earth. Your eyes could see me as an embryo, but in your book all my days were already written; my days had been shaped before any of them existed."

Psalms 139:13-16

(CJB)

FIFTEEN

"WHY ME? WHY YOU?"

*M*any times over the past sev-
eral years, I have often wondered, "Why God?
Why me? Why us? Aren't there those who are
better qualified? Those who are more talented?
Those who are more educated? And God, what
about those who have it all together? Not like me,
who's a mess most of the time. What about them?
Why is this required of me? Who am I? I'm a
nobody. I'm insignificant!"

Pity party? Maybe! Yet sometimes what God calls us to do can appear very overwhelming. So overwhelming that without His supernatural wisdom and infinite knowledge, how could anyone deal with or handle certain situations He leads us into. Those impossible events that rattle our very foundation and make us question our talents, our wisdom, our knowledge and even our calling.

The Bible says that before we were conceived in our mother's womb, before we were even thought of, God fashioned our days and nights. He knew about our ups and downs; our faults and failures; our giftings and talents; our abilities and inabilities.

The Bible also says that the steps of a righteous man are ordered of the Lord. That means that if I love the Lord and follow His commandments and teachings, then He is in control of my steps.

What a comforting thought! He knows who I am! He fashioned my days and nights! He knows what I can do and what I can not do! He knows when I have it all together and when I'm a mess! He knows when I feel strong or when I feel insecure! He knows everything about me -- and still He uses me!

Why me? Why us? Maybe it can be best explained with a song that my grandfather wrote many, many years ago.

THEY NAILED HIM TO A TREE

If a king should come from Heaven,
Robed in ivory, gold, and pearl,
With the Glory of an Angel,
When He came into this world.
Would the people glad receive Him,
Or rejected would He be,
Would they honor Him as Leader,
Or would they nail Him to a tree?

(Chorus)
They nailed Him to a tree,
They nailed Him to a tree.
They nailed my Blessed Savior to a tree.
He filled the Father's plan,
And died for every man,
And has a home in Glory now for me.

Jesus never came for Glory,
Yet of Glory He was King,
He came to banish sorrow,
That deliverance He might bring.
He came to sinners rescue,
To set the captive free:
But in purple robes they put Him,

And they nailed Him to a tree.

Dear Jesus came from Heaven,
The humblest, of men,
He lived a life of burden,
Just to free the world of sin;
But they numbered Him transgressor,
Blasphemer was the plea;
And they crowned Him with the sinner,
And they nailed Him to a tree.
(Frank L. Kellogg, 1920)

Jesus Christ sacrificed His life for you and me. He came to bring deliverance to people and He was misunderstood. He was mocked, laughed at, criticized and never accepted as Leader and King. He gave all He had and held nothing back. Being that He is our example, why should we think He wouldn't require the same of us?

Those in ministry pay a high price. The price is your life! The sacrifice is great -- that of friends and family. The cost is everything you have. Sounds like what Jesus did when "They Nailed Him to a Tree."

If He is our example, and He is, can we then ask, "Why me? Why us?" or should we say, "Thank you Lord for the journey you took to the tree. And thank you for being with us through our

"Why Me? Why You?"

journey through ministry."